SACRED SONG OF THE HERMIT THRUSH

A Native American Legend

by Tehanetorens

Illustrated by Jerry Lee Hutchens

THE BOOK PUBLISHING COMPANY
SUMMERTOWN, TENNESSEE USA

WITHDRAWN

Tribal Library
Saginaw Chippewa Indian Tribe
7070 E. Broadway
Mt. Pleasant MI 48858

ISBN 0-913990-36-1

Printed on 100% post-consumer recycled paper

The Book Publishing Company
PO Box 99
Summertown, TN 38483 USA

Copyright © by Tehanetorens

Illustrations by Jerry Lee Hutchens

ALL RIGHTS RESERVED. No part of this book may be reproduced or utilized in any form or by any means, electronic or mechanical, including photocopying or by any information retrieval system without permission in writing from the publisher.

Tehanetorens
    Sacred song of the hermit thrush / by Tehanetorens : illustrated
by Jerry Lee Hutchens
            p.   cm.
      ISBN 0-913990-36-1 : $5.95
      1. Mohawk Indians—Legends. 2. Hermit thrush—Folklore.
3. Birdsongs—Folklore. I. Title.
E99.M8T44 1993
398.2'089973—dc20   93-945
                                                CIP

2

Tribal Library
Saginaw Chippewa Indian Tribe
7070 E. Broadway
Mt. Pleasant MI 48858

PUBLISHER'S FOREWORD

Tehanetorens is a master story teller. His words provide us with another way to see the world.

Ideally, the best way for a story to be communicated is in the Old Way — elders gathered with their younger relatives, during the colder months, educating each other within the family circle. A book can only convey a part of the richness of a story such as this. However, since stories are not told so often in these days, this book is presented as a stepping-stone, to fix a story in memory. When the readers are elders they may gather around their young and not-so-young relatives for a session of story-telling, thus keeping this knowledge and tradition alive in the hearts of the People for still another generation.

DEDICATION

The story of the Hermit Thrush was first published in pamphlet form by the Akwesasne Mohawk Counselor Organization. The original dedication read: "We, the Akwesasne Mohawk Counselor Organization from the St. Regis Reservation dedicate this pamphlet, 'How Hermit Thrush Got His Song', to the noted historian and author, Mr. Hale Sipe of Freeport, Pennsylvania. We dedicate this little forest tale to Mr. Sipe because in all his writings, he has written the truth concerning the old time Indian. He has not tried to cover up or hide true Indian history. As this honest historian says: 'It is a historian's duty to record the wrongs committed upon the Indian, as well as the wrongs committed by him. History must not hide the truth.' We are grateful to Mr. Hale Sipes, a true historian and a real friend, for the attitude he has taken."

TABLE OF CONTENTS

SACRED SONG OF THE HERMIT THRUSH

Long ago, the Birds had no songs.
Only Man could sing, and every morning,
Man would greet the rising Sun with a song.

The Birds, as they were flying by,
would often stop and listen
to the beautiful song of Man.
In their hearts they wished
that they too could sing.

8

One day,
the Good Spirit
visited the Earth.

The Good Spirit walked over the Earth
inspecting the various things he had created.
As he walked through the forest,
he notice that there was a great silence.
Something seemed to be missing.

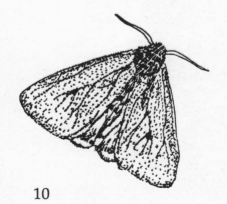

11

As the Good Spirit pondered,
the sun sank behind the western hills.
From the direction of the river,
where there was an Indian village,
there sounded the deep rich tones of an Indian drum,
followed by the sacred chanting of the sunset song.
The Good Spirit listened.
The song was pleasing to the ears of the Good Spirit.

12

13

The Good Spirit looked around.
He noticed that the Birds were also
listening to the singing.
"That is what is missing!" said the Good Spirit.
"Birds should also have songs."

The next day, the Good Spirit called
all of the Birds to a great council.
From near and far they came.
The sky was filled with flying birds.

16   The trees and bushes bent to the earth under the weight of so many.

On the great Council Rock sat the Good Spirit. He waited until all of the Birds had perched and had become quiet.

The Good Spirit spoke. He asked the Birds if they would like to have songs, songs such as the People sang.

17

With one accord, the Birds all chirped,
"Yes! Yes!"

"Very well," said the Good Spirit.
"Tomorrow when the Sun rises in the East,
you are all to fly up in the Sky.
You are to fly as high as you can.
When you can fly no higher,
you will find your song.
That Bird who flies the highest will have
the most beautiful song of all the Birds."

Saying these words,
the Good Spirit vanished.

Next morning, long before sunrise, the Birds were ready.
There was great excitement.
However, one little Bird was very unhappy.
It was the little brown Hermit Thrush.
Perched beside him was Akweks, the Great Eagle.
As the little Bird gazed at the Eagle he thought,
"What chance have I to compete with this great Bird?
I am so little and Eagle is so large.
I will never be able to fly as high as he."

As he was thus thinking, an idea entered his mind.
"Eagle is so excited that he will not notice me."

With this thought in mind,
the Hermit Thrush flew like a flash
to the Eagle's head.
Quickly he hid under Akwek's feathers.
The great Eagle was so excited
that he did not notice the little Thrush.

"With my great wings, I will surely win," said the Eagle.

The Sun finally looked over the eastern hill.

With a great roar of wings,
the many Birds took off.

For a long time, the Birds flew upward.
Finally, the smaller, weaker birds began to tire.
The little Hummingbird was the first to give up.
His little wings beat the air so hard
that to this day one can, if one listens,
hear his humming wings.
His little squeaking call says,
"Wait, wait for me," a very plain song.

26

The fat Cowbird was the next to give up.
As he floated down, he listened and
heard his song, a very common song.
Other Birds weakened
and while flying eastward,
listened and learned their songs.

At last, the Sun was
at the end of the Earth.
The Night Sky
began to darken the Earth.
By this time, there were only a few Birds left.
They were the larger, strong-winged Birds:
the Eagle, Hawk, Owl, Buzzard, and Loon.
All night, the Birds flew up,
ever up.

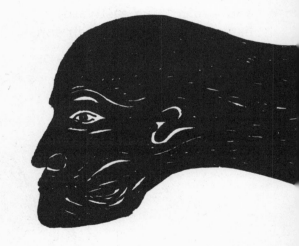

28

When the Sun rose next morning,
only the Eagle,
chief of all Birds,
was left.
He was still going strong.

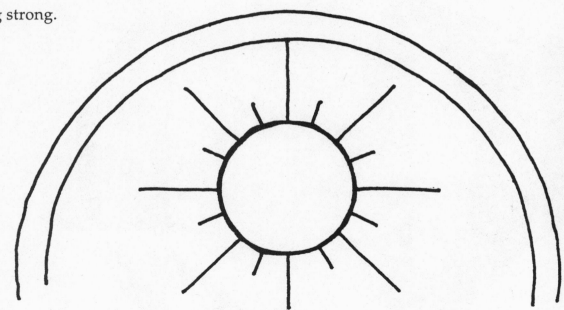

31

When the Sun was
halfway in the Sky,
Eagle began to tire.
Finally, with a look of triumph,
for there were no other Birds in sight,
the tired Eagle began to soar Earthward.
The little Thrush, riding under the feathers of the great Eagle,
had been asleep all of this time.
When the Eagle started back to Earth, little Thrush awoke.
He hopped off the Eagle's head and began to fly upward.

33

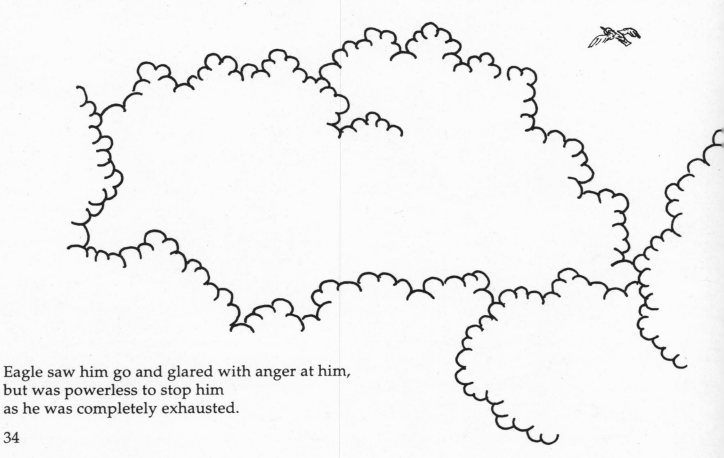

Eagle saw him go and glared with anger at him,
but was powerless to stop him
as he was completely exhausted.

35

The little Thrush flew up and up.
He soon came to a hole in the Sky.
He found himself in a beautiful country.
As he entered the Spirit World, he heard a beautiful song.

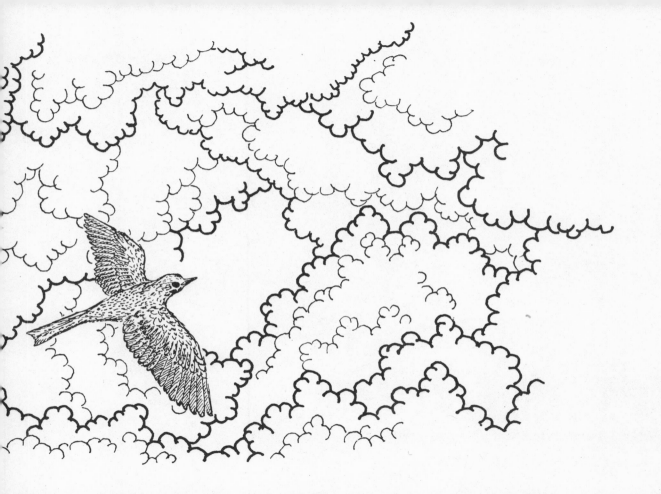

He stayed in Heaven for a while learning this song.

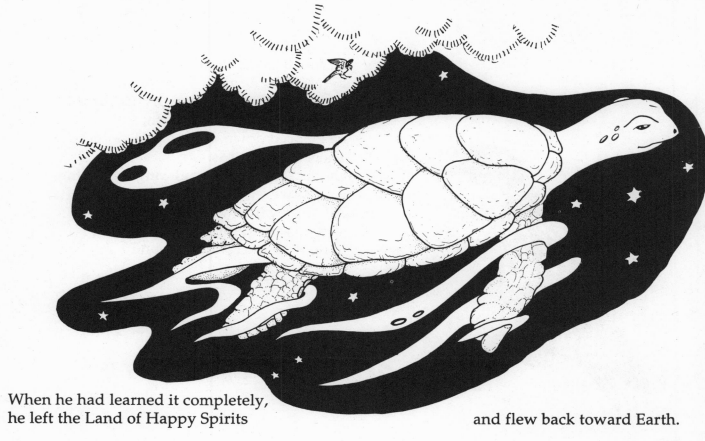

When he had learned it completely,
he left the Land of Happy Spirits

and flew back toward Earth.

Hermit Thrush could hardly wait
to reach the Earth.
He was anxious to show off his beautiful song.
As Thrush neared the Earth,
he glanced down at the Council Rock.
There sat the Birds.
On the Council Rock, glaring up at him
was Akweks, the Eagle.
All of the Birds were very silent
as they waited for Thrush
to light on the council ground.

41

Suddenly, the feeling of glory
left the little Thrush,
and he felt ashamed.
He knew he had cheated
to get his beautiful song.
He also feared Akweks,
who might get even with him
for stealing a free ride.
He flew in silence
into the deep woods.
In shame,
with dragging heart,
he hid under the branches
of the largest Tree.
He was so ashamed
that he wanted
no one to see him.

There you will find him today.
Never does the Hermit Thrush
come out into the open.
He is still ashamed because he cheated.
Sometimes, however,
he cannot restrain himself
and he must sing his beautiful song.
When he does this,
the other Birds cease their singing.
Well they know that
the song of the Hermit Thrush,
the song from the Spirit World,
will make their songs very weak.
That is why Hermit Thrush is so shy.
That is why his song
is the most beautiful song of all the Birds.
That is why this Spirit Song
causes the Sun to shine
in the hearts of the People who hear it
as they go into the dark forest.

NATURAL HISTORY OF THE HERMIT THRUSH

by Jerry Lee Hutchens

The hermit thrush was familiar to the Original People of this continent. There was an understanding born of companionship in a shared environment. Europeans and their descendents have been slow to understand the hermit thrush. The famous painter/ornithologist, John James Audubon, wrote that the hermit thrush has no song at all! It is interesting to see how different cultures shape an individual's perceptions. One man is surrounded by the songs of Spirits where another finds only silence. The song of the hermit thrush is truly a song from the Spirit World, sacred sounds relayed to gladden our hearts and join us to the feathered beings who share our time on the earth.

Walt Whitman shared this understanding when he wrote of the hermit thrush:
> Sing on there in the swamp,
> O singer bashful and tender, I
> hear your notes, I hear your
> call.
> I hear, I come presently, I
> understand you.
> — from *When Lilacs Last in the Dooryard Bloom'd*

The migratory patterns of the hermit thrush have been established over eons. Thrushes first appear in the fossil record during the Miocene Epoch over seven million years ago. As a distinct species, the hermit thrush probably emerged during the last 2,500,000 years as four major ice ages moved up and down the North American continent. Each fall hermit thrushes migrate from Canada and New England down to Tennessee, where I live. Some don't settle until they reach the Mayan homelands in the hills of Guatemala; others spend the winter here.

I saw one on a day in late November. We were along the Hatchie River at a place dominated by tall leafless oaks. A feeder creek flowed through an opening of young pine and maple. The bird had all the special marks of the hermit thrush: speckled breast, rusty rump and tail. The tail swung up and down in a measured arch that is characteristic of the hermit. The hermit thrush doesn't sing in winter, but as I watched him work his way up the branches of a white oak, I though silently, "Beautiful Bird, I am working on a book about your sacred song. Please sing for me." The thrush lifted his head and sang. In the grey chill of winter he sang the song from the Spirit World. Then it was time to say, "Thank you," which I did.

Still, I wasn't hearing all the sounds of the song. Other hermit thrushes hear those phrases too high for human ears. They contain subtleties known only to thrushes and the Good Spirit that instructs them.

As the seasons move from winter into spring, the increasing hours of daylight generate remarkable changes in the thrush. These changes are not triggered by light entering the eyes. Instead, the light passes through the thin skull of the hermit and directly stimulates photo-receptor cells living on the surface of the brain. The bird's brain increases hormone production, stimulating the part of the brain that regulates singing. This small fluid-filled cavity in the forebrain is lined with immature, specialized neuron stem cells. These cells climb up thin threads of tissue called radial glia. At the end of their climb the newborn neurons come to rest in the high vocal center of the male, the part of the brain used for singing. The center begins to grow, signaling the beginning of the mating season when song becomes most important to birds.

The growth of new brain cells in an adult bird parallels the embryonic development of human brains. New neurons in the developing human fetus are spawned in brain cavities and then climb the fibrous cells of the radial glia. The radial glia pathways determine the shape and structure of the brain. In humans the brain reaches its fullest construction by birth and the fibers retract. Without the fibers to climb, no new brain cells grow. If a person's brain is damaged by disease or accident, the part of the brain that dies is gone forever. In the male hermit thrush, the radial glia stay in place, allowing neurons to climb the fibrous ladder to singing success. The bird's ability to grow new brain cells for singing holds clues that may one day help millions of brain-damaged humans.

How is the hermit physically able to produce such a beautiful song?

Long ago, Europe was covered with dense forests. In the shadowed realm lived tribal people with enchanted stories of the woodland spirits. One story tells of a beautiful nymph spirit named Syrinx. Her loveliness excited a great longing in Pan, a man-like forest god with goat's feet and horns. Syrinx spurned Pan's love. Pan tried to catch her on the banks of a stream, but grabbed only a handful of hollow reeds instead. His heavy breathing over the reeds produced a magical sound. To this day, a flute, called a syrinx, is made of a bundle of reeds.

Syrinx is also the name given to the hermit thrush's vocal organ. The syrinx is located at the bottom of the windpipe and controlled by pairs of tiny muscles. The hermit thrush's ability to sing the song of the Spirit World comes from these muscles controlling the tension on the membranes of the syrinx as air passes over them. The bird is able to control the right and left sides of the syrinx separately and thus sing with two independent voices.

A song as complex and lovely as the hermit's holds many layers of meaning. The song can define territory, individuality, location, health and status. Females notice many things about a male's song. Mates are chosen from the best singers; there is a genetically programmed sense for good music. The beautiful singing leads to pair bonding and nest building.

Nesting sites are commonly near swamps or the steep banks of streams, especially in moist spruce or other evergreen forests. Occasionally, hermit thrushes are forced out of their favorite habitat by wood thrushes. In these cases, the hermit is likely to move into drier pine-oak woodlands.

The nest is made on the ground or low in a tree. Unlike many other monogamous birds, only the female hermit builds the nest. She employs rotted wood, sticks, moss and grass. On occasion a middle layer of mud is used. The final lining of fine mosses, rootlets or pine needles serves to insulate and cushion the eggs.

The hatching of a young bird from the egg is a time of incredible transition. For twelve or so days the incubating hermit embryo swims in liquid albumen or egg white. Just before hatching, the young bird swallows the liquid and stores the water in its body tissues. Any unused yoke is pulled into the unhatched bird's body. This yoke is used as a food source for a time after hatching. At the blunt end of the egg, an airspace enclosed in a membrane has formed. The youngster pierces the membrane with its beak and begins breathing the air in the sac. In this way the lungs are quickly prepared for full operation.

This is a period of great vulnerability. Squirrels, racoons and skunks will eat unprotected eggs. Owls, hawks and many hungry mammals devour the young, who are born blind, naked and helpless. The hatchlings require twelve days to grow a full set of feathers. After the feathers have grown, the young leave the nest. Now they begin the behavior associated with adulthood, such as bathing, migration and "anting."

"Anting" is any process a bird uses to collect the defensive secretions of ants. The high humidity of the hermit thrush habitat provides a moist environment favorable to the growth of molds and fungi. Ant secretions have documented fungicidal abilities. Birds may hold one or more worker ants in their beaks and rub the insects on their feathers and skin. The thrush does not do this with just any ant. It avoids species of ants that sting and selects ants that ooze or spray formic acid. Ant defensive secretions also kill tiny insects, mites and bacteria. Deer ticks, the carriers of Lyme disease, like to hitch rides on birds. It is probable that anting by birds reduces the spread of Lyme disease. In this way, the hermit thrush also protects human life.

Regular bathing is an important part of the hermit's life. The skin is exposed by fluffing the feathers and flicking the wings in and out of the water. The breast is stuck down into the water and swished around. Coming up, the head is thrown back so water douses the back.

When humans breathe, the oxygen is passed into tiny lung sacs called alveoli. The thin walls of the alveoli allow oxygen to pass through and enter the blood stream. In birds, oxygen gets two passes through the lungs. Inhaled air first goes through the lungs and then into air sacs in the hollow bones and elsewhere in the body. When the air leaves these sacs, more oxygen is harvested by the lungs. This gives the birds more energy for flying and singing.

This oxygen-rich blood is pumped to all parts of the body by a powerful heart beating hundreds of times a minute. Rapid movement of blood functions to regulate the body temperature between 106° F and 114° F and the feathers serve as insulation. The hermit thrush can tolerate fairly cold temperatures. Still, it migrates south as winter comes on. This is mostly because the food supply is reduced as insects go dormant and fruits cease production.

The digestive system of the hermit thrush is very efficient at rapidly assimilating food. Like people, the hermit thrush has taste buds on its tongue and the back of its throat. Although it has fewer taste buds than people, it can distinguish the same tastes as humans. In the spring and summer the hermit feasts on insects, spiders and worms. In fall and winter the hermit thrush feeds on wild grapes, juniper berries, dogwood, staghorn sumac and poison ivy.

Fruit-eating birds like the hermit are important to the fruit-producing plant. Many fruit bushes and trees need birds to spread their seeds. Plants regulate bird feeding in several ways. In order to have as many seeds as possible, the plant makes the fruit only nutritious enough to get the birds eating them. If the fruit were any less nutritious, the birds would starve and the plant's seeds would not be spread. Greater nutrition would take plant energy out of seed production. Generally, the fruits are green and bitter until the seeds are ripe. When the seeds are ready, the plant floods the fruit with sugars, turning them red, yellow or another showy hue. These colors alert the bird that the food is ready. After eating the fruit, the bird passes the seed in fertilizer-rich droppings. In this way, the hermit thrush plays a role in maintaining the precious balance of life.

We can never completely know the forest and its creatures, but we can have a full experience of the mystery of life. The hermit thrush with its enchanted song communicates that mystery.

A portion of all sales of
Sacred Song of the Hermit Thrush
go to support the Akwesasne Freedom School.

AKWESASNE FREEDOM SCHOOL

The Akwesasne Freedom School is an independent elementary school, grades pre-K - 5, run by the Mohawk Nation. Akwesasne, "the land where the partridge drums," is located on the St. Lawrence River in upstate New York. The school was founded in 1979 by Mohawk parents concerned that their language and culture would slowly die. In 1985 a Mohawk language immersion program was begun, the only program of its kind in the United States. The Akwesasne Freedom School combines solid academics with a strong foundation in Mohawk culture. Students study reading, writing, math, science, history and the Mohawk ceremonial cycle.

PURPOSE

The Mohawks have been losing their language, culture and identity for many years. The Akwesasne Freedom School was formed to help make the Nation strong again by focusing on the young people. "The children are the backbone of the nation" is a common Mohawk saying. Their survival depends on their ability to preserve old ways and cope with the new. The school is a reversal of the assimilation process which has absorbed so many Native Americans into modern non-Native culture.

The prophecies say that the time will come when the grandchildren will speak to the whole world. The reason for the Akwesasne Freedom School is so the grand-children will have something significant to say.
— Sakokwenionkwas (Tom Porter), Mohawk Chief

Language is the key to preserving the culture. Chief Tom Porter estimates that 90 percent of adults over forty are fluent in Mohawk, yet only 5 percent of teenagers and 1 percent of preschoolers now speak Mohawk as a primary language. The Akwesasne Freedom School is fighting to reverse these statistics through its language immersion program.

It is very important that we learn our culture and ceremonies. Without this we wouldn't be where we are today. We would be just as destructive to our environment as other societies. We give thanks to the foods, trees, grasses, water and everything that gives us strength to survive. We shall always continue to keep our ceremonies because if we do not, we will eventually take advantage of Creator's great gifts to us.

— *Katsitsiakwas, Freedom School Graduate*

Mohawk leaders not only serve their communities, but travel the globe bringing the message of the Peacemaker: We must all live in harmony with one another and with all living things, and the influence of each action must be considered for seven generations of unborn children. Through Mohawk language and ceremony, the Akwesasne Freedom School strives to develop traditional leaders and future ambassadors.

CURRICULUM

The Thanksgiving Address, used to open all traditional Mohawk gatherings, is the foundation for the curriculum. It provides guidelines for learning respect and giving thanks to the Creator and to all creation. It teaches that creation has a spirit and is a living being. Each school day is opened and closed by one of the students giving the Thanksgiving Address in Mohawk from memory. Thus, each student is trained to be a public speaker.

Language is the key to cultural survival. Because language exists in a social and cultural context, the school teaches it thematically. A general introduction is given to vocabulary, semantics and syntax. Language is learned through speaking, singing, writing and reading. The final semester is taught in English to ease the transition to public schools, where federal funds provide only one-half hour of Mohawk language instruction daily.

Mathematics is taught in a program similar to that in public school. All basic skills, including the metric system, are covered.

Science is taught with the goal that students will develop the skills and attitudes necessary for making wise decisions about the future. The child's curiosity and awareness are developed by studying the areas mentioned in the Thanksgiving Address: health and medicines, grasses, trees, animals, birds, water, wind, Thunder, Sun, the Moon and the Earth.

History and geography are taught to help students understand their way of life from physical, historical, economic and human views. Both traditional ceremonial and contemporary events are examined.

Kanien'keha:ka Aohsera, or the Mohawk Ceremonial Year, is a vital part of students' education. The students go to the Longhouse to celebrate the Traditional Fifteen ceremonies. These are the only holidays during the school year.

Below is the ceremonial cycle:

1. Midwinter
2. Dead Feast
3. Tobacco Burning
4. Maple Tree
5. Thunder Dance
6. Medicine Mask
7. Seed-Planting
8. Strawberry
9. Raspberry
10. Beans
11. Green Corn
12. Harvest
13. Thunder Dance
14. Dead Feast
15. End of Season

FUNDING

Funding for the Freedom School comes primarily from the parents. Eighty percent of the operating budget for fiscal year 1988 came from the community of Akwesasne: 10 percent from tuitions of $1,000 per family and 70 percent from fundraisers, including an annual quilt auction and chicken dinner, a survival race, concerts, lasagne suppers, car washes and t-shirt sales. The remaining 20 percent comes from donations by individuals and foundations. In-kind donations by parents, the community and friends covered much of school maintenance, special activities and fundraising costs.

The Viola White Water Foundation, headquartered in Harrisburg, Pennsylvania, is the tax exempt fiscal sponsor of the school. It was founded in 1977 by Jimmy Little Turtle to raise funds for Native American education and culture, including such Mohawk nation projects as *Akwesasne Notes*, an indigenous newspaper, and the Freedom School. Donations ear-

Tribal Library
Saginaw Chippewa Indian Tribe
7070 E. Broadway
Mt. Pleasant MI 48858

marked for the school and made to the Viola White Water Foundation are tax deductible.

> Viola White Water Foundation
> 4225 Concord Street
> Harrisburg, Pennsylvania 17109
> (717) 652-2040

Your help is needed now at the Akewsasne Freedom School. Through the knowledge and understanding the children gain of their people's traditions, important values are nurtured, such as self-respect, community and kinship with the natural world. The Akwesasne Freedom School prepares the children to live confidently in the larger American society while preserving their Native heritage for future generations. The students become spiritually and politically aware, making them proud of who they are and more understanding of the peoples of the world.

A Natural Education $5.95
Basic Call to Consciousness $7.95
Blackfoot Craftworker's Book $11.95
Children of the Circle $9.95
Dream Feather $11.95
A Good Medicine Collection:
    Life in Harmony with Nature $9.95
How Can One Sell the Air? $6.95
Indian Tribes of the Northern Rockies $9.95
Legends Told by the Old People $5.95
The People: Native American Thoughts and Feelings $5.95
The Powwow Calendar $6.95
Sacred Song of the Hermit Thrush $5.95
Song of Seven Herbs $10.95
Song of the Wild Violets $5.95
Spirit of the White Bison $5.95
Teachings of Nature $8.95
Traditional Dress $5.95

These fine Native American books
are available
from your local bookstore or from:

THE BOOK PUBLISHING COMPANY
PO Box 99
Summertown TN 38483

Please include $2. per book
additional for shipping.

If you are interested in other fine books
on Native Americans,
ecology, alternative health, gardening,
vegetarian cooking and children's books,
please call for a free catalog:

1-800-695-2241